Reading Hebron

By Jason Sherman

Playwrights Canada Press
Toronto • Canada

Reading Hebron © Copyright 1996 Jason Sherman
Playwrights Canada Press
54 Wolseley St., 2nd fl. Toronto, Ontario CANADA M5T 1A5
Tel: (416) 703-0201 Fax: (416) 703-0059
e-mail: cdplays@interlog.com   http://www.puc.ca

Playwrights Canada Press publishes with the generous assistance of The Canada Council for the Arts - Writing and Publishing Section and the Ontario Arts Council.

Playwright photo by Cylla von Tiedemann.

Canadian Cataloguing in Publication Data
Sherman, Jason, 1962 —
        Reading Hebron

A play
ISBN 0-88754-533-5
I. Title.
PS8587.H3858R42 1997   C812'.54   C97-930298-6
PR9199.3.S43R42   1997

First edition: July 1997.
Printed and bound in Winnipeg, Manitoba, Canada - Hignell Printing Ltd.

Playwright's Acknowledgments

Thanks to producer David Duclos - Under the Umbrella Festival.

Thanks to Artistic Director Peter Smith and General Manager Rebecca Scott - Playwrights' Workshop Montreal.

Thanks to The Canada Council for the Arts and the Toronto Arts Council for their generous financial assistance.

A very special thanks to Brian Quirt, who pushed, pulled, prodded and provoked, and deserves much more credit than is revealed by the words director-dramaturge.

Jason Sherman's other plays include *Three in the Back,
Two in the Head; The Retreat; The League of Nathans;*
and *None Is Too Many*. His work has received a
Governor General's Literary Award for Drama, a
Chalmers Award and the Canadian Authors' Association
Award for Drama. He is working on *Patience* for
Tarragon Theatre, *It's All True* for Necessary Angel
Theatre Company, and *A Short Tale About Animals* for
Theatre Direct, as well as two radio drama series for
CBC Radio, *P.M.O.* and *National Affairs*. Jason
Sherman has been a playwright-in-residence at Tarragon
Theatre in Toronto, since 1992.

Playwright's Production Notes

Doubling: The actor playing Nathan plays no other roles. Two men and two women are needed for the remaining roles, as follows:

FIRST MALE	SECOND MALE	FIRST FEMALE	SECOND FEMALE
Judge 1	Witness 2	Witness 1	Judge 2
Consul reception	Judge 3	Judge 4	Lotte
Witness 4	Lev	Jan	Witness 3
Witness 5	Judge 6	Judge 5	Mom
Witness 8	Witness 7	Randa	Witness 6
Said	Leibowitz	Judge 8	Judge 7
Clerk	Mr. Big	Jane	Boss
Rosenthal	Conspirator	Secretary	Ashwari
Excited Man	Lerner	Ex-wife	Mossad agent
Zaydie	Spielberg	Ozick	Settler 4
Mourad	Sternberg	Eliach	
Mossad agent	Dad	Bubbie	
Settler 2	Mossad Agent	Ben	
Rabin	Chomsky	Mossad agent	
	First Hasid	Second Hasid	
	Settler 1	Settler 3	
	Baruch	Noa	

I would advise against anything approaching naturalism in the staging. The play requires nothing more than a desk and a few chairs. Dany Lyne, who designed the first production, created a multipurpose table accompanied by a bench and twin chairs which served all our needs — the bench, for example was used as a seat in Mr. Big's office, a bed in the Boss' house, and a bookshelf in the bookstore.

Props, also, should be kept to a minimum. Other than books, magazines, newspapers and files, the play needs a bottle of wine here and a set of candlesticks there. The actors should wear the same costumes throughout (with an occassional accesory, if desired) so that the actors — not their outfits — create the different characters.

The line breaks and absence of punctuation in the Judges scenes are an attempt to slow down the testimony, to make the delivery more deliberate, less overtly emotional and almost devoid of interpretation. The more controlled the delivery, the more powerful the testimony. There should be a great contrast between these scenes and all the others.

Quotation marks around a character's name indicates that Nathan is imagining this part of the conversation in the midst of a real conversation; it's best if the audience thinks the conversations between Nathan and the Isreali consulate receptionist and the Palestinian receptionist are continuous — no special lighting tricks to give the game away. After the library scene, where Jane is both a real and an imaginary person, the quotation marks are dropped, since, by now, it should be clear that Nathan is making things up.

Speaking of Nathan's fantasies — such as the ones he has in the library and the bookstore — these should be staged as seamlessly as possible, so that characters appear out of "nowhere".

Accents are entirely appropriate throughout — the more outrageous the better, except in the Judges scenes, where moderation would be prudent.

Edward Said last name is pronounced sah-eed.

There is no intermission. Playing time should be about 85 minutes.

I've kept the stage directions to a minimum.

Reading Hebron was first performed as part of the Theatre Centre's Under the Umbrella Festival in Toronto, in January, 1995, with the following cast:

Liza Balkan
Michael Healey
Earl Pastko

Director-dramaturge - Brian Quirt.

Reading Hebron was expanded and presented in a series of public readings at Playwrights' Workshop Montreal in April, 1996, with the following cast:

Michael Healey
Niki Landau
Joel Miller
Felicia Shulman-Rowat
Robin Wilcock

Director - Lise Ann Johnson.
Dramaturge - Brian Quirt.
Stage Manager - Anne Clark.

Reading Hebron was produced by Factory Theatre in Toronto, November 20th to December 8, 1996, with the following cast:

Michael Healey
Niki Landau
Alon Nashman
Earl Pastko
Felicia Shulman

Director-dramaturge - Brian Quirt.
Assistant director/stage manager - Naomi Campbell.
Set and costumes - Dany Lyne.
Lighting - Paul Mathiesen.

Judges I

> *Nathan Abramowitz's apartment. A desk, on
> top of which sits a telephone, and nothing
> else.*
>
> *NATHAN enters with a stack of books,
> magazines, files, newspapers.*

NATHAN   (*addressing the audience*) On February 25th, 1994,
Dr. Baruch Goldstein, a settler from Kiryat Arba,
committed a massacre at the Tomb of the
Patriarchs in Hebron. On February 27th, 1994, the
Government of Israel decided to appoint a
Commission of Inquiry to determine whether
Goldstein acted alone or with accomplices.

The telephone rings.

Hello?...No, I...I can't talk right now.

He hangs up.

The Commission heard most of the testimony in
sessions that were open to the public.

The Commission held 31 sessions and heard
evidence from 106 witnesses, some of them at the
Commission's initiative and some at their own
request.

The complete or partial testimony of 16 witnesses
was heard behind closed doors.

The Commission made a public announcement
requesting that anyone who wished to testify
before it or present it with documents or exhibits,
make their intention known to it in writing.

The placement of the judges and witnesses is up to the director — the first production had them at windows behind an upstage wall that extended from one side of the stage to the other.

JUDGE 1
The witness
is a settler
from Kiryat Arba
near Hebron
You are a reservist
with the Israeli Defense Forces

WITNESS 1
Yes

JUDGE 1
And you were on active duty
the morning of the massacre

WITNESS 1
Yes
I was at a
communications headquarters
in Kiryat Arba
At 5 a.m. I received a call
from Dr. Goldstein
He asked that I meet him
at his clinic
and take him down
to the Tomb of the Patriarchs

JUDGE 1
Did he give any indication
of what he was about to do

WITNESS 1
No hint
No
We talked a little
about ambulance supplies
for the settlement
Oh
I proposed a way
to keep intravenous infusions warm
He said
"I hope there won't be any more need
for infusions"
He cared very much
about human life

JUDGE 2	The witness is the army commander for the West Bank
WITNESS 2	For Judea and Samaria that is correct
JUDGE 2	Would you tell us what happened at the Tomb of the Patriarchs on February 25th 1994
WITNESS 2	At 5.20 a.m. Dr. Goldstein entered the mosque in his army uniform
JUDGE 2	He carried his weapon in plain view
WITNESS 2	Jews Only Jews are permitted to bring in weapons with them
JUDGE 2	He carried a bag with him
WITNESS 2	Yes We can assume that it contained the ammunition magazines
JUDGE 2	Why was the bag not checked
WITNESS 2	It is policy not to inspect bags carried by Jews
JUDGE 2	Even though it is standard in almost all public buildings in Israel for people to be asked if they are carrying weapons and to have bags searched
WITNESS 2	Dr. Goldstein did not receive special attention didn't arouse suspicion He told an officer who knew him that he was on reserve duty In a section of the Tomb known as the Isaac Hall

400 to 500 Muslims
were beginning their Ramadan Friday prayers
In the adjacent Abraham Hall
13 Jews were reciting prayers for Purim
Dr. Goldstein entered the Isaac Hall
through the first of three doors
then fired into the worshippers
from different locations at the back of the hall

JUDGE 2

Where were the Israeli soldiers
who were supposed to be on duty

WITNESS 2

Three of them had slept in
and arrived when it was all over
A regular policemen was also not there
and another soldier
had been sent by a superior officer
to switch places with a soldier outside

JUDGE 2

So only one of the six Israelis
assigned to the security detail
was in place

WITNESS 2

That is correct

JUDGE 2

How did he react to the gunfire

WITNESS 2

He tried to make his way into the hall
but was pushed back by the crowd
trying to escape
He finally made his way into Isaac Hall
but it was too late
He found Dr. Goldstein dead
in a corner
beaten by the Palestinians
with a fire extinguisher

JUDGE 2

Can you tell us General
why Jews are permitted
as a matter of routine
to bring weapons to the cave
when Palestinians do not enjoy
the same privilege

WITNESS 2   It dates back to 1980
                   after an Arab attack
                   that killed six Jews in Hebron

JUDGE 2   What do you make of the policy

WITNESS 2   I think it makes sense
                   The firearms have been a deterrent
                   to Arab violence

JUDGE 2   Why this discrimination

WITNESS 2   I would not draw conclusions
                   from an extraordinary case
                   of a lunatic
                   God forbid
                   I could have found myself testifying
                   before a commission
                   after Jews were butchered
                   by 500 inflamed Muslim attackers
                   Then the question would have been
                   why weren't the Jews armed
                   when they were praying
                   so close to 500 Muslims

JUDGE 2   I do not understand why people
                   who are coming to pray to God
                   have to take weapons with them

WITNESS 2   I don't have an answer to that
                   Those were the decisions
                   The thing that is hard for me to imagine
                   Is that in a place where there are armed soldiers
                   a Jew
                   an Israeli
                   would do such a thing

Paranoia

NATHAN makes a telephone call, the consulate receptionist answers.

CONSULATE   (*on the telephone*) Shalom, Consulya Israel.

NATHAN   Oh, oh. Hebrew.

CONSULATE   Israeli Consulate, hello.

NATHAN   (*on the telephone*) Oh, hello. I'm looking for information about the Hebron Massacre.

"CONSULATE"   Why?

NATHAN   Um. I'm a...rabbi and. It's a research project.

"CONSULATE"   (*outrageous Israeli accent; over the top*) BULLLLLLSHEEEEEEEEEEET!

NATHAN   Okay. Look. I'm a Jew. I'm *interested*. I'm worried the whole thing's gonna be passed off as the work of a madman.

"CONSULATE"   It *was* the work of a madman. Goldstein was a foreign implant, a Brooklyn Jew who went to Israel to kill Arabs.

NATHAN   But—

"CONSULATE"   You think you're the only Jew disgusted by what he did?

NATHAN   No, but—

"CONSULATE"   There are plenty of Jews hanging their heads in shame and remorse over this unforgiveable atrocity. But do we go around trying to slander the whole Jewish race?

NATHAN   I'm not trying to—

"CONSULATE"   You're out to *prove* something, admit it.

NATHAN   No, I just want to make sure I understand it all.

"CONSULATE"   Understand it all? If you want to understand it all, you better do more than read about Hebron. You can't take some isolated event, forget about history, ignore the fact that a month before the massacre, Goldstein watched a close friend of his die at the hands of an Arab terrorist.

NATHAN   The Palestinians are an occupied people.

"CONSULATE"   And that gives them the right to *kill Jews?*

NATHAN   I'm not condoning terrorism on either side.

"CONSULATE"   Then why pick on the Hebron Massacre? Read *today's* paper. Any more suicide bombings? You ought to be ashamed of yourself, ashamed to call yourself a Jew. What is it with you, why is it everytime an Arab dies you run screaming bloody murder, and every time a Jew is killed you call it self-defense. What is wrong with you?

NATHAN   I don't have an answer to that.

CONSULATE   Sorry to keep you waiting. Can I help you?

NATHAN   Yes. I was wondering, is there someone there who could help me get some information about the inquiry that was held recently into the massacre at Hebron.

CONSULATE   Yes, I can help you. What were you looking for?

NATHAN   Oh. Just. Do you have a copy of the report?

CONSULATE   I have a copy of excerpts, in English. You're more than welcome to it. Do you have a fax?

NATHAN	No. Could I pick it up?
"CONSULATE"	Certainly. I'll leave it at deception.
NATHAN	Sorry?
CONSULATE	Certainly. I'll leave it at reception. Your name?
NATHAN	My name. Is. Nathan Abramowitz.
"CONSULATE"	I *figured* as much. Hey, Lotte.
"LOTTE"	Yeah?
"CONSULATE"	I got Abramowitz on the line. Don't worry, *Nathan,* we've got a *file* on you. We know who you are, anti-Semite, self-hating Jew...
"LOTTE"	(*checking the file*) Kapo.
"CONSULATE"	Kapo...
"LOTTE"	Sondercommando.
"CONSULATE"	Sondercommando...
"LOTTE"	Betrayer of your race.
"CONSULATE"	Betrayer of your race.
"BOTH"	...ASSIMILATIONIST!
NATHAN	What?!
"CONSULATE"	Married a shiksa didn't you? Two boys, neither one circumcised.
NATHAN	That was for medical reasons!
"CONSULATE"	Christmas trees? Easter egg hunts? Are those for medical reasons, too?
NATHAN	I'M STILL A JEW!

CONSULATE   ...Alright, Mr. Abramowitz. I'll leave it at
                 reception. When will you pick it up?

NATHAN   Today. Four o'clock?

CONSULATE   We close at three today. It's shabbas.

NATHAN   Of course it is. Yes. Two o'clock then.

CONSULATE   It'll be waiting for you.

                 He tosses the report to NATHAN.

Judges 2

JUDGE 3

The witness
was a soldier at the Tomb
We heard testimony
that you were stationed by a door
in a passageway
and that as worshippers fled
you fired six or seven shots
into the air

WITNESS 3

We fired not only into the air
but also at the door

JUDGE 3

How many shots
did you fire at the door

WITNESS 3

At least four

JUDGE 3

How high

WITNESS 3

Some were chest high
But no one was hit
by our bullets

JUDGE 3

How can you be certain

WITNESS 3

The worshippers
hadn't reached the door yet
If I'd hit somebody
I'd have seen him fall

JUDGE 3

Why did you fire

WITNESS 3

At first
we thought that a Palestinian was shooting
inside the mosque
and we wanted to stop him from reaching us
They would have trampled us

So we shot at the door
before any of the worshippers got there
We wanted to create a jam at the door
We were afraid that the shooter
if he was an Arab
would come outside and hurt us
We stopped firing
when we saw a wounded man stagger out of the
mosque
He was full of blood
We understood
that a Jew was firing inside
not an Arab
and that they were fleeing for their lives

JUDGE 4

The witness
was in the Jewish prayer area
Can you describe what you heard

WITNESS 4

I heard several closely-spaced bursts of gunfire
The bursts sounded like they were coming
from the same weapon
We
the Jewish worshippers
took cover
We were afraid of an Arab attack
or fighting among the Muslems
Some of us fled
But the army told us to go back
So we went back
and continued our services

JUDGE 4

You continued your prayers

WITNESS 4

Yes
For an hour
It was Purim
after all

JUDGE 4

Did you
or any of the others
know
what had happened in the mosque area

WITNESS 4   No
             I didn't
             When I got back home
             I heard what had happened on the radio

JUDGE 4   Thank you

WITNESS 4   May I say
             that I am grateful
             that no other Jews were hurt
             in the incident

JUDGE 4   No other Jews

WITNESS 4   In addition to Dr. Goldstein
             Thank God
             it all ended well

Hi Mom

The telephone rings.

NATHAN	Hello?
MOM	Hello, darling.
NATHAN	Hi, Mom.
MOM	What's doing?
NATHAN	Same as yesterday when you called.
MOM	So: what time you coming Tuesday?
NATHAN	Tuesday?
MOM	Passover. You forget or something?
NATHAN	No.
MOM	I want to sit by seven.
NATHAN	Alright.
MOM	So you'll come when?
NATHAN	Seven?
MOM	So late?
NATHAN	Six-thirty?
MOM	Your cousin Jan's gonna be here.
NATHAN	Jan...
MOM	From Israel. With Lev.

NATHAN	Who?
MOM	Her husband. They're very anxious to talk to you.
NATHAN	Oh?
MOM	They know how interested you are in Israel.
NATHAN	Uh huh.
MOM	So come a little early.
NATHAN	What are they um...anxious about?
MOM	They didn't...they just...they want to talk to you.
"LEV"	You got no right to say ONE WORD about ISRAEL!
"JAN"	Lev, please...
"LEV"	NEVER MIND "Lev please." You think we need your lousy money? Mr. Big Shot North American Jew.
"JAN"	Don't make trouble.
"LEV"	Who's making trouble, I'm talking. You try living with Hezbollah rockets landing in your backyard, wondering are your children going to be blown up. We're building a country here for the Jewish people and the day you make aliyah is the day you'll be a Jew, and not before,
NATHAN	Alright, I'll come up at six.
MOM	Don't do me any favours.
NATHAN	Mom...
MOM	I wouldn't mind a little help setting up.
NATHAN	Five-thirty.
MOM	We got 15 people coming.

NATHAN	Five o'clock.
MOM	The way my back's feeling, I don't think I'm gonna be able to stand long...
NATHAN	Uh huh.
MOM	...make the matzah balls...
NATHAN	Yeah.
MOM	...carve the brisket...
NATHAN	Mmhm.
MOM	...vacuum.
NATHAN	Why don't I come up Monday and sleep over?
MOM	Alright.
NATHAN	I'm kidding, Mother. Okay, look. I'll come up at four.
MOM	Four...
NATHAN	I'm working next Tuesday.
MOM	You're gonna work Yontif?
NATHAN	'Scuse me. (*silent scream*) Mom. The office closes at three. I'll be up at four.
MOM	Fine. Are you bringing the boys?
NATHAN	I don't think so.
MOM	Why not?
NATHAN	It's better this way.
MOM	Mm. Well, it's up to you.
NATHAN	I gotta go.

MOM   If it was up to me.

NATHAN   I really gotta go. Goodbye.

MOM   Goodbye.

        They hang up.

Judges 3

JUDGE 5
The witness
was at prayer in the mosque
What can you tell us about the attack

WITNESS 5
It began with an explosion that shook the hall
Then there was gunfire
and another blast
We heard more than one source of shooting

JUDGE 5
In your earlier statement
to investigators
following the massacre
you made no mention
of multiple sources of gunfire

WITNESS 5
When Goldstein took out an empty clip
firing continued
from another source

JUDGE 5
Did you in fact see a second shooter

WITNESS 5
No
I was shot
I was lying on the floor
waiting to be carried out
Also the overhead lights had been shot out
so the room was in darkness
People were trying to get out
some wounded
others
carrying the bodies of the dead
They reached the passageway
screaming for help
trying to pull soldiers inside
to help the wounded and dying
When I was carried out
there was shooting

from many directions
from many sides

JUDGE 6   The witness
was in the women's section of the mosque

WITNESS 6   When I got out of the women's section
I tried to get into the room
where the massacre had taken place
I could see the three soldiers by the door
with their guns
I could not get into the mosque
There were too many people
Suddenly
I heard gunfire
and I saw one of the soldiers
firing at the people
I saw one man
run toward a soldier
and yell
"God is great"
The soldier shot him

JUDGE 6   That is all

WITNESS 6   I want to say
something else
There are
half a million Arabs
in the Hebron area
Either they will have to go
to the Arab states
or the troublemakers
the settlers
will have to be moved out

JUDGE 6   Thank you

WITNESS 6   I hope the commission
will be neutral
and that it will achieve
positive results

Palestine House

NATHAN makes a telephone call.

RANDA	Palestine House.
NATHAN	Yes. Hello. Is that Palestine House?
RANDA	Yes.
NATHAN	Good. Um. Do you have a library or a resource centre of any kind?
RANDA	We have a small library, yes.
NATHAN	Good. Because I'm looking for documents related to the…Hebron Massacre? Have, have you heard of the Hebron Massacre?
"RANDA"	Of course. What do you know about it?
NATHAN	Well. Just what I've read.
"RANDA"	Precisely. What you've read. You have no experience with our situation. You would shit your pants if you ... ... had to leave the comfort of your cozy world and live amongst us.
NATHAN	I don't deny that for a second. The point is…
"RANDA"	The point is that for you, it's an intellectual pursuit. "The effect of the massacre on the soul of the Jewish people. How could a Jew commit this stain upon us?" To think that a Jew, who is essentially a good person, could commit such a crime. Now an Arab, well, naturally, an Arab, who is essentially a violent person, would do this. But a Jew?

NATHAN   No. Look. You've got this all wrong. What I'm
                saying is, let's not whitewash the Hebron
                Massacre, let's not write it off as another action of
                a deranged madman, but look at it as proof of
                Jewish racism, and and and deal with that, I mean,
                let's take a good hard look at ourselves for once,
                and drop the rhetoric and the bullshit and for once,
                for once leave the Holocaust out of it and say,
                "Look, a great injustice has been done, we took
                another people's land, we have become the
                oppressor, we have murdered, we have tortured, we
                have lied, and it is time to DO SOMETHING
                ABOUT IT."

                RANDA applauds. The others join in.

NATHAN   Thank you. Thank you. No. No, please.

"RANDA"   Nathan Abramowitz, ladies and gentlemen!

NATHAN   Thank you. No, no, thank *you.*

"RANDA"   Nathan Abramowitz! Saviour of the Palestinian
                people!

NATHAN   Alright.

"RANDA"   You see, Nathan, you are not truly interested in
                the plight of the Palestinian people. We are
                merely a pet project; you think you are a
                humanist, that you believe in justice for the
                underdog, so you point fingers in the direction of a
                land to which you have never been, and you say
                "That is no way to act." And this, despite the fact
                that you would act no differently if it were you.

NATHAN   That's not true.

"RANDA"   Isn't it? The revolution begins in your own home,
                Nathan. Do you treat those around you with
                respect and dignity?

NATHAN   So let me see if I got this straight. You have no
                reports or documents or…

RANDA	We only have a small library here. Have you tried the Metro Reference?
NATHAN	Metro Reference.
RANDA	Or the Israeli Consulate?
NATHAN	Uhh...
"RANDA"	Why don't you try them. You see we're just a welcome house for terrorists.
NATHAN	Sorry?
RANDA	I say, we're just a welcome house for immigrants. So we don't really have anything about the Hebron Massacre here.
NATHAN	Yeah. Well, that's typical. You know how hard it is for me to find Palestinian literature? You know, you people have to do a better job of getting the message out.
"RANDA"	I know, but we are so stupid.
NATHAN	Apparently.
"RANDA"	And badly organized.
NATHAN	This too is true.
"RANDA"	All we know how to do is blow up buses. I don't know why we don't just go and live in Jordan. That is our country. But no. We stay. We want to spend our lives making bombs and living in squalid refugee camps, with shit and piss running through the streets. We are cowards; we are not to be trusted; we stink; we are ugly; we don't even exist, really. Why, if it were not for the work of good people like you, we would disappear altogether. I say," Thank Allah for people like Nathan, without whom the Palestinian people would be helpless. We are so grateful to you, Nathan, for wanting to help us."

Pause.

NATHAN   Thanks, I...thanks.

RANDA   Sorry I can't be of more help. Why don't you
                  leave me your name and number and if I find
                  anything I'll—

NATHAN   No, that's okay, thanks. I'll try the library.

He hangs up.

Judges 4

JUDGE 7

The witness
is a senior noncommisioned officer in Hebron
What did you understand your orders to be
regarding shooting at settlers

WITNESS 7

My orders were never to fire at a settler
even if he is shooting at other people

JUDGE 7

What would happen
if you saw a settler
shooting a woman
a child
a civilian

WITNESS 7

It depends on the situation
If I had seen him shooting
one or two shots at someone
I wouldn't have shot to kill him
immediately
But if it was a
massacre
or something
it depends
The directive says not to shoot

JUDGE 7

Even if you see that it is a massacre

WITNESS 7

Even if I see that it is a massacre
the directive of the brigade commander
is not to shoot

JUDGE 7

What do you think of this directive

WITNESS 7

I find it
surprising

JUDGE 8

The witness
was West Bank commander in 1992 and '93
We have heard from several witnesses
that Israeli forces in the West Bank
have standing orders not to fire at settlers
even if they are shooting at Palestinians or troops

WITNESS 8

On the question of firing at Jews
in connection with disturbances
the answer was perfectly clear
It discriminated between
Jews and Arabs
Absolutely clear discrimination
which is also understandable
Arab riots often endangered soldiers' lives
so they were allowed to fire
in some cases

Regarding Jews
of course there is discrimination
Even in the most serious confrontations
between soldiers and Jews
it did not occur to anyone
I hope
that a Jew would even injure a Jewish soldier

So in cases of disturbances
there was an absolute prohibition to open fire
Even shooting tear gas
to disperse a Jewish demonstration
required the approval of the division commander

JUDGE 8

What if a soldier
were to see
a settler firing

WITNESS 8

Army orders
were that the soldier was not to shoot
because the natural situation
is that a Jew is defending himself
against Arab attack
No-shoot orders did not apply
by the way
to murderous Jewish assaults

JUDGE 8   Is it possible
               that the orders were interpreted
               in that way by soldiers

WITNESS 8   It should be clear to soldiers
               that they must open fire
               if necessary
               to prevent life-threatening crimes
               However
               no such directive was drawn up for such situations
               because nothing like this massacre
               could have been anticipated

Nathan at Work

NATHAN is now at his office job. The first two times THE BOSS calls for NATHAN can be overlapped with WITNESS 8's last speech.

BOSS	Nathan. Nathan. Hey, Nathan.
NATHAN	Huh?
BOSS	You still here?
NATHAN	No. I'm a hologram.

She laughs.

BOSS	The office is closed.
NATHAN	Right. I just, uh, I wanted to type up those minutes for ya.
BOSS	Forget about the minutes.
NATHAN	Tomorrow's my last day.
BOSS	Forget about the minutes.

Pause.

BOSS	Lemme ask you something. I mean, do you mind…?
NATHAN	No, no.
BOSS	Well. You're Jewish, right?
NATHAN	Right.
BOSS	What are you doing for Passover?

NATHAN   I'll, I'm going to my mom's house for dinner.

BOSS   Oh yeah? That's nice.

NATHAN   Yeah.

BOSS   Yeah.

NATHAN   Yeah yeah…well, goodnight

BOSS   Nathan.

NATHAN   Uh huh?

BOSS   I was wondering if. Well. You do good work.
            You're punctual and pleasant and everybody around
            here seems to like you.

NATHAN   I hardly know what to say.

BOSS   You came in, you told a joke or two. Really lifted
            the place up.

NATHAN   I'm blushing all over.

BOSS   All over?

NATHAN   Tick tock.

BOSS   What I'm getting at is this: how'd you like to stay
            on, full time? A regular salary. Bonuses. The
            whole schmeer.

NATHAN   I don't think so.

BOSS   Are you telling me you'd rather temp all your life?
            Go from one job to the next, never settle?

NATHAN   I don't like staying in one place too long.

BOSS   Why's that?

NATHAN   I'm sensitive to smells.

BOSS   So what are you gonna do?

NATHAN	I don't know. Travel.
BOSS	Really? Where to?
NATHAN	Israel.
BOSS	I love Israel. Oh my God, so much history.
NATHAN	So I've heard.
BOSS	And the people. They really, they know who they *are,* you know? So confident. They really live in the moment, you know? Nathan?
NATHAN	Mm?
BOSS	You ever been?
NATHAN	To Isra—no.
BOSS	Hold old are you, Nathan?
NATHAN	Early thirties, I'd say.
BOSS	Uh huh. Married?
NATHAN	I think I was.
BOSS	I don't get you.
NATHAN	Me neither. I should go now.
BOSS	Nathan. What is it? What's on your mind?
NATHAN	It's hard to pin down. Oh wait, I remember now. Endless human suffering. Gets me right here. I'm torn between wanting to change the world and wanting to blow it up.
BOSS	What are you gonna do about it?
NATHAN	Worry.
BOSS	And?

NATHAN   Complain.

BOSS   What are you doing tonight?

NATHAN   Tonight? Going to bed.

BOSS   And after that?

NATHAN   Waking up. Going to bed. Waking up. It's
                endless.

BOSS   Nathan. My home number. (*stuffing a piece of
                paper into NATHAN's shirt pocket*) Call me if
                you get lonely.

                BOSS exits.

NATHAN   *Get?*

The Library

*NATHAN goes to the Metro Reference
Library.*

JANE   Can I help you?

NATHAN   Yes, I was wondering if—

                The telephone rings.

JANE   'Scuse me.

                Metro Reference...You want the history
                department, I'll put you through. (*to NATHAN*)
                Can I help you?

NATHAN   Yes, I was wondering if you could tell me—

                The telephone rings.

JANE   Metro Reference...thirteen. Okay.(*to NATHAN*)
                Can I help you?

NATHAN   Yes, I was wondering if you could tell me why the
                Hebron Massacre is different from all other
                massacres.

JANE   ...The what.

NATHAN   The Hebron Massacre.

JANE   Spell it.

NATHAN   Uh. N-A-T-H-

JANE   What?

NATHAN   Oh. Sorry. H-E-B-

The telephone rings.

JANE	Metro Reference…what?…no we don't. (*she hangs up*)
"JANE"	(*taking an interest in NATHAN*) Hi…Can I…help you?
NATHAN	Yes. I'm looking for information about the Hebron Massacre.
"JANE"	Oh. You interested in…?
NATHAN	Well I'm. I've been following it in the papers…
"JANE"	*Papers…*
NATHAN	Yeah, *The New York Times* had—
"JANE"	*New York Times,* are you kidding, that lapdog of the rich and powerful, for*get* it, if you want the *real* story, you have to get your hands on as much information as you can. You have to dig *deep.*
NATHAN	I already *have* a lot of information. I just, I feel like there's something I'm not *getting.*
"JANE"	Have you read Edward Said?
NATHAN	No.
"JANE"	Oh, you have to *The Question of Palestine!* Brilliant insights into the nature of Palestinian identity.
SAID	(*appearing out of nowhere*) Please, you flatter me.
"JANE"	Professor Sa*id.* May I introduce…
NATHAN	Nathan Abramowitz. Pleasure to meet you, sir.
SAID	Not at all.
"JANE"	Nathan's looking for information on the Hebron Massacre.

SAID   I see. Well. I was not surprised by it. I visited
                  Hebron two years before the massacre, and was
                  shocked to find, even then, heavily armed Israeli
                  soldiers inside the mosque. I felt that a Muslim
                  holy place had been violated, deliberately, and that
                  Hebron was simply waiting to explode.

NATHAN   I'm so glad to talk to you. I've been trying to get
                  the Arab...

JANE   Ahem.

NATHAN   I mean Palestinian, point of view. But I haven't
                  had much luck.

SAID   Of course not. Arabic literature is heavily censored
                  in the democratic West; as for Palestinian writing,
                  well, I'm afraid we haven't done a very good job
                  of creating our own narrative.

"JANE"   Why don't you ask Professor Said a question?

NATHAN   Professor Said, if and when you are invited to
                  speak to Jewish audiences, what will you tell
                  them about the future of Jews in Palestine?

SAID   My goodness—what a powerful question that is! It
                  is very difficult for me to talk about the future of
                  another people, which feels itself, for the most
                  part, to be so different from the Arab Palestinians.
                  But the Palestinian experience is a struggle to
                  achieve a mode of coexistence. Over the last
                  generation a strong bond has been formed between
                  the Israeli and the Palestinian on the basis of fear.

ASHWARI   I think the Israelis have allowed themselves to fall
                  victim to the psychology of the occupier, where
                  you study the occupied only for the purposes of
                  domination and control.

"JANE"   Nathan, may I introduce Hanan Ashwari, Minister
                  of Education for the Palestinian Authority.

NATHAN   Ms Ashwari.

"JANE"   Oh, and you should read *The Fateful Triangle*.

SAID &
ASHWARI   Ahh...Chomsky.

"JANE"   And there's an interview with Yeshayahu Leibowitz in *Tikkun*...Mr. Leibowitz won the Israel Prize, "for a lifetime of original thought and social criticism," but he turned it *down*.

LEIBOWITZ   The reasons were personal, not ideological. I was fed up with the uproar. People were upset about my positions.

"JANE"   Tell him.

LEIBOWITZ   Israel is going through a Nazification process. The problem we face is that there are many people who are enamoured of being Jewish, of their Jewishness — but for them this has no connection with Judaism. So this becomes a nationalism that quickly falls into idolatry and self-deception. Israel is not a state of Judaism — it is simply a secular state whose problems have nothing to do with Judaism.

                The telephone rings; JANE goes to get it.

NATHAN   Wait. Don't answer that.

"JANE"   Why not?

NATHAN   I need some answers.

"JANE"   There are no answers, Nathan. Only positions. What's yours? (*they all stare at NATHAN, waiting for an answer, the telephone rings*) Metro Reference...let me check. Can I help you?

Mr. Big

The scene switches to the office of Mr. Big (in fact, a loan officer at NATHAN's bank). For the switch JANE can hand the library telephone to the actor playing LEIBOWITZ, who then becomes MR. BIG. NATHAN's first line is then in response to JANE's last line.

NATHAN   I'm here to see Mr. Big.

SECRETARY   I'll see if he's in.

NATHAN   Never mind, sister.

SECRETARY   Hey! Stop! You can't go in there! Security!

                NATHAN bursts in on MR. BIG, who's on the telephone, chomping on a cigar.

NATHAN   Put the telephone down.

MR. BIG   (*into the telephone*) Hold on a second, will you Bill?

SECRETARY   I'm sorry, Mr. Big, he just walked right past me.

NATHAN   I said put the phone down, now.

MR. BIG   It's alright, Lotte. I've been expecting you, Nathan.

NATHAN   Expecting me?

MR. BIG   Have a seat. Go back to your desk, Lotte.

                She exits.

MR. BIG   Nathan, please. Sit. I'll be right with you.

NATHAN sits; MR. BIG returns to his telephone call.

MR. BIG   Mr. President? Listen, I have to go, I've got Abramowitz here...that's right...that's right...oh don't you worry about that...a ha ha ha...you just worry about those loan guarantees...uh huh......well, if you think losing Israel as a strategic ally is...then you know what to do...alright...I'll wait for your call. Love to Chelsea.

He hangs up.

MR. BIG   Drink?

NATHAN   No thanks.

MR. BIG   I'm surprised it took you this long to find me.

NATHAN   It wasn't easy. I had to read *The Fateful Triangle.*

MR. BIG   Ah...Chomsky.

NATHAN   Israel, the United States and the Palestinians: the fateful triangle.

MR. BIG   Yes, I've read it. Let me see: Israel is a client state of the US; they have a symbiotic relationship— Israel gives the US a strategic presence in the Middle East, originally as a buffer against Soviet aggression, later to stem the tide of Islamic terrorism; the US, in return, pours billions of dollars of military and economic aid into Israel and protects it from international censure; thus, US interests are served, Israel self-destructs and the Palestinians get it in the neck. That about it?

NATHAN   A little simplistic, but...

MR. BIG   But essentially, that's it?

NATHAN   Yes.

MR. BIG	And since the government of the United States is nothing more than a puppet regime for those who own the country — General Motors and the like — the Middle East situation is the result of market forces too complex for most people to understand.
NATHAN	They'd understand it if the media had the guts to point it out once in a while.
MR. BIG	Oh sure, sure kid, the media, yeah, I-I-I forgot, they're all part of this, too. But ultimately, the bloodshed is the result of the Chairman of General Motors serving the needs of his stockholders.
NATHAN	Damn right.
MR. BIG	The Israelis, the Palestinians, they're all pawns in the game.
NATHAN	Precisely.
MR. BIG	Well. You have connected the dots quite thoroughly. There's only one dot you've left out.
NATHAN	Oh?
MR. BIG	Yours. After all, you have a decent life.
NATHAN	Some would say.
MR. BIG	You seem to work fairly regularly.
NATHAN	Often as I can.
MR. BIG	You support two children.
NATHAN	I do.
MR. BIG	Yet you have no stocks or bonds.
NATHAN	None.
MR. BIG	RRSP?

NATHAN	Negligible.
MR. BIG	Mutual funds?
NATHAN	Morally opposed.
MR. BIG	Short term investments.
NATHAN	Zip.
MR. BIG	I see.
NATHAN	You see?

The telephone rings.

MR. BIG	Yes?
SECRETARY	David Frum on two.
MR. BIG	Take a message. Still, you have all the necessities.
NATHAN	True.
MR. BIG	A standard of living most of the world envies.
NATHAN	A standard of living made possible by exploiting most of the world.
MR. BIG	I suppose you'd be happy in a shack. Guilt, Nathan. That's all it is. You know, I don't think we're all that different, you and I.
NATHAN	Except I'm sitting on this side of the desk and you're sitting on that side of it.
MR. BIG	Would you like to sit on this side?...Please. Just for a moment.

They switch seats.

MR. BIG	How's that feel?
NATHAN	Not so bad.

MR. BIG	You're in control now, Nathan. Go ahead. Fix it. Give the world a makeover. What are you gonna do first?
NATHAN	Redistribute the wealth.
MR. BIG	Good.
NATHAN	End corporate welfare.
MR. BIG	Uh huh.
NATHAN	Establish a Palestinian homeland.
MR. BIG	Of course.
NATHAN	And Native self-government.
MR. BIG	Why not hand the whole country back to the Indians? After all, we stole it from them, herded them into camps, infected them with diseases, destroyed their culture, reduced them to streetcorner drunks.
NATHAN	Now you're talking.
MR. BIG	Fine. Well. That's it then.
NATHAN	What a day.
MR. BIG	There's just one more thing you ought to do.
NATHAN	Uh huh.
MR. BIG	Change human nature. Take away our awareness of death. Our instincts for envy, hate, greed, revenge, power... Go on, Nathan. Rage against the machine. Sign a petition. Go on a march. Get yourself a foster child. Listen. The day you walk in here ready to acknowledge that you are motivated by your very real fear of being alone, and not by some vague hope for solidarity, that is the day I will break bread with you. On that day, I will call you friend. And give you anything you ask for. Anything else, Mr. Abramowitz?

> *MR. BIG becomes the loan officer at this point — his cigar now a fountain pen — as NATHAN snaps back to reality.*

MR. BIG   Mr. Abramowitz?

NATHAN   No.

MR. BIG   It's not that I don't *want* to extend your line of credit.

NATHAN   It's just a thousand dollars.

MR. BIG   I understand that but, Mr. Abramowitz, look at it from where I'm sitting. You haven't held a steady job in five years. You have no assets.

NATHAN   There are no steady jobs, Mr. Loan Officer. I'm doing the best I can. I temp.

MR. BIG   It's unpredictable.

NATHAN   So's life.

MR. BIG   Pardon?

NATHAN   For example.

> *NATHAN strangles the bank manager.*

Die. Die. Die.

MR. BIG   I'm afraid I can't do that.

> *NATHAN leaves.*

Israel's Books

NATHAN goes to a Jewish bookstore.

CLERK   Can I help you find something?

NATHAN   Yes. I'm looking for anything to do with the Hebron Massacre.

CLERK   Which one?

NATHAN   Which...one?

CLERK   There've been so many. In 1929, the Arabs murdered 60 Jews.

NATHAN   I was thinking about 1994.

CLERK   Of course you were. Well. There aren't any books that deal specifically *with* that. Amos Oz wrote an essay about it, and there are a couple of others that mention it in passing.

NATHAN   Alright.

CLERK   That's the problem with Israel. You talk about one event, you wake up the next day, they're onto something else

NATHAN   *Plus ça change.*

CLERK   If you're interested in the wider context of the Palestinian question, I could recommend a few titles.

NATHAN   Sure.

The telephone rings.

CLERK	One second. (*picking up*) Israel's Books and Tapes...Lotte? Just a second...(*to NATHAN*) I'll just be a minute, why don't you have a look around...(*into telephone - this continues under following, diminishing in volume until it fades right out; as he speaks, the CONSPIRATOR enters, loaded down with books*) Well I just talked to him...I don't know what he's looking for...he seems very confused...uh huh...and the children?...what, he's going to turn them against us, too?...it's terrible...
CONSPIRATOR	Pssst.
NATHAN	Hm?
CONSPIRATOR	You interested in Hebron?
NATHAN	Yeah, I—
CONSPIRATOR	Keep your voice down.
NATHAN	Yes. I'm interested.
CONSPIRATOR	I happen to know a thing or two about it.
NATHAN	Uh huh.
CONSPIRATOR	Come over here...you can't be too careful. You hear about Yayha?
NATHAN	Who?
CONSPIRATOR	*Yayha.* From Hamas. The one who planned the suicide bombings. Mossad got him. Blew his head off. With a cell phone. *He has a big laugh as he looks around the room.* They can get you anywhere. Now listen. This Hebron thing. You don't understand.
NATHAN	I know, I'm trying—

CONSPIRATOR   Shhh. Listen. It's bigger than Hebron. Goldstein, he's nothing you understand? He's like the Watergate plumbers. The inquiry, the judges, they're going to pass him off as a madman. If you ask me, it's the judges who are crazy, if they—

A customer passes by.

IF THEY THINK THE LEAFS ARE GOIN' *ANY*WHERE THIS YEAR THEY'RE CRAZY. THEY'RE NUTS THEY'RE...

The customer has left.

The settlers think they're following their destiny as laid out in the Bible.

NATHAN   That's why call the West Bank Judea and Samaria.

CONSPIRATOR   Ten points, bubbie. For them everything has biblical significance. They're fighting a holy war. See? It's not political; these fuckers are serious. They think the West Bank is theirs from thousands of years ago. And it's not just the settlers. This goes back to Ben Gurion. The Zionist dream was to reclaim all the of ancient Israel. The Israelis don't care that they've displaced the Palestinians. As far as they're concerned, the Palestinians were never there. Golda Meir said, "they did not exist."

The customer who passed by earlier, who has been looking at NATHAN, turns out to be COUSIN JAN.

JAN   Nathan?

CONSPIRATOR disappears behind a bookcase.

Oh my God! Lev! Lev, it's Nathan.

LEV   (*emerging from behind the bookcase; awkwardly*) Hello.

JAN	You don't remember me? What's my name? What's my name? Cousin...
NATHAN	Cousin...
NATHAN & JAN	Jaaaaaan!
JAN	Nathan, this is my Lev, my husband.

Pause.

| LEV | We hear so much about you. |

Pause.

JAN	Well, we have to run.
NATHAN	Me too.
LEV	I'll bring the...the...(*indicates car*)

He exits behind the bookcase.

| JAN | We'll see you at your mom's? |
| NATHAN | Absolutely. |

She exits. CONSPIRATOR reappears.

CONSPIRATOR	"Cockroaches," that's what Sharon called them. "Two-legged beasts." "Palestinian" is synonymous with "terrorist." All Goldstein's doing is carrying the policies of Israel to their logical conclusion. And those of us who watch it happen are as guilty as Goldstein, because we're allowing it to happen.
NATHAN	What can we do?
CONSPIRATOR	That depends. Are you prepared to be called an anti-Semite? That's how they get you.
NATHAN	I'm ready.
CONSPIRATOR	Alright.

The CLERK has snuck up behind them.

CONSPIRATOR	Don't look at me. Look ahead. They're watching us.
NATHAN	Who?
CONSPIRATOR	Mossad, schmuck.
NATHAN	Where?
CONSPIRATOR	Look ahead. Laugh. Ha ha ha.
NATHAN	Ha ha.
CONSPIRATOR	Now. What's the root word of Hebron?
NATHAN	Um um um
CONSPIRATOR	Haver.
NATHAN	Haver.
CONSPIRATOR	Haver. And what did Clinton say on hearing of the death of Rabin?
NATHAN	Um um um.
CLERK	Shalom Haver.
CONSPIRATOR	So Shalom Haver means?
NATHAN	Hello Hebron.
CONSPIRATOR	Or?
NATHAN	Peace Hebron.
CONSPIRATOR	Or?
NATHAN	Goodbye Hebron.
CONSPIRATOR	Exactly!
NATHAN	Goodbye Hebron!

CONSPIRATOR   Now—who signed the Oslo Accord?

NATHAN   Arafat.

CONSPIRATOR   And?

NATHAN   Rabin.

CONSPIRATOR   Good. And the Accord calls for Israel to pull out of Palestinian towns, right?

NATHAN   Right.

CONSPIRATOR   And what's the last town from which the army was to pull out?

NATHAN   Hebron.

CONSPIRATOR   Right again. And who stalled that pullout? Don't look at me!

NATHAN   Sorry!

CONSPIRATOR   Laugh.

NATHAN   Ha ha.

CONSPIRATOR   Well?

NATHAN   Netanyahu.

CONSPIRATOR   Good. And what is his nickname?

NATHAN   Bibi.

CONSPIRATOR   And what do you think of when you think of the word "bibi"?

NATHAN   A gun?

CONSPIRATOR   Exactly! You see! It all fits! You must take a gun, go to Hebron and kill Benjamin Netanyahu. Only then will there be peace. Go, Nathan. Kill Netanyahu.

> *The CLERK grabs the CONSPIRATOR from behind.*

CLERK   One more word and you die. You feel that? One more word and I shoot you through your self-hating Jewish heart.

CONSPIRATOR It's up to you now, Na—

CLERK   I said shut up. Let's go. You first. Nice...and slow, see...that's...the way to do it...nice...and slow.

> *They exit. The CLERK returns.*

CLERK   Did you find what you were looking for?

NATHAN   Uh huh.

CLERK   (*looking at the books NATHAN picked up*) *Israel: A Colonial-Settler State.* A classic in the field. *Zealots for Zion.* Very revealing. *Chronicles of Dissent.* Ah. Chomsky. A brilliant man. But between you and me? Self-hating Jew.

NATHAN   Thanks. I'll take 'em.

Moral Equivalence

> *NATHAN returns to his apartment, with an*
> *armful of books and magazines. The*
> *telephone is ringing.*

NATHAN   Hello?

EX-WIFE   It's me. Your ex-wife.

NATHAN   Yes?

EX-WIFE   Not that I'm desperate to speak with you.

NATHAN   Uh huh.

EX-WIFE   But if you could return just one of my phone calls.

NATHAN   I've been a little busy.

EX-WIFE   With what?

NATHAN   Things.

EX-WIFE   Things, right, and I guess these "things" are more important than Ben and Andrew.

NATHAN   What are you talking about...

EX-WIFE   I'm talking about...

NATHAN   ...they were just here.

EX-WIFE   Yeah, watching cartoons.

NATHAN   They watched "Pinocchio" a couple times, what's—

EX-WIFE   Uh huh.

NATHAN   What's wrong with that?

EX-WIFE   Nathan, you've—

NATHAN   What is wrong with *that?*

EX-WIFE   You've got to spend time with them.

NATHAN   I.

EX-WIFE   You want them to grow up without knowing you?

NATHAN   Look—*no.*

EX-WIFE   Then?

NATHAN   I can't talk about this right now.

EX-WIFE   You can never talk about *this* right now. You think just because you moved out it's all gonna go away?

NATHAN   That was the plan, yes.

EX-WIFE   You can't pretend I don't exist. I mean we lived together a long time, Nathan. We had kids together for Christ's sake.

                ASHWARI enters. In the first production, she entered at an upstage window.

ASHWARI   Think of the terrible effect this is having on our children.

NATHAN   Don't *use* the kids, *please.*

ASHWARI   They suffer. I begin to feel responsible for all the children killed by the Israelis.

NATHAN   Okay, look. I'll spend more time with them.

EX-WIFE   That's all I'm asking. You going to your mom's tomorrow?

NATHAN   Yeah.

EX-WIFE	Say hi to everyone.
NATHAN	Will do.
EX-WIFE	I'm gonna miss it this year.
NATHAN	Goodbye.

He hangs up; starts sorting through the material he's picked up on his travels - there should be an overwhelming amount of material. After a while:

NATHAN	Step up to the microphone, please. State your name.

As he flips through the books and magzines, people appear out of nowhere. Stars of David are lit against the back wall, and gaudy music - a bar-mitzvah band's "Hava Nagila", perhaps - plays thoughout.

LERNER	Michael Lerner.
NATHAN	And what do you do?
LERNER	I'm a writer. I edit a magazine called *Tikkun,* which is a journal of opinion on Jewish uhh matters.
NATHAN	A left-wing journal, would it be safe to say?
LERNER	Left-wing, yes, alright.
NATHAN	Alright, Mr. Lerner, and you have something to say about the Hebron Massacre?
LERNER	Yes. Yes, I do.
NATHAN	Alright. And the title of your speech?
LERNER	Is "Disarm the West Bank Settlers."

NATHAN   You'll be judged on originality, economy of
                language and humour. You'll have thirty seconds
                to make your points. At the twenty-five second
                mark, you'll hear this sound (*he imitates the sound
                of a bomb whistling to its mark*) at which point
                you'll be asked to wrap up. If you exceed the five-
                second mark, you'll hear this (*the bomb explodes*),
                at which point you'll have to stop. Alright?

LERNER   Got it.

NATHAN   Michael Lerner, with "Disarm the West Bank
                Settlers." Thirty seconds, starting...now.

LERNER   (*quickly*) The murder of more than 40 Palestinians
                at Ramadan prayer in a mosque in the West Bank
                town of Hebron yesterday cannot be dismissed as
                the action of a psychopath and nothing more. Yes,
                Dr. Baruch Goldstein, a religously observant
                Yeshiva University graduate who was armed with
                an automatic rifle, was crazy. But his craziness
                mirrors a climate of hatred nurtured by right-wing
                Jews who, raised on a steady diet of Holocaust
                stories and anti-Arab racism, are determined to
                show that Jews can be powerful—even if that
                power can be exercised only against an unarmed
                and essentially defenseless Palestinian population.
                North American—

                The sound of a whislting bomb.

NATHAN   Five seconds.

LERNER   North American Jews who wish to dissociate
                themselves from the extremists must insist that
                the Israeli Army disarm all West Bank and Gaza
                settlers.

NATHAN   Well done, Michael Lerner. We'll see you again
                for the quick-fire round at the end of the show.
                Next speaker, step up to the mike. Your name?

ROSENTHAL   A.M. Rosenthal.

NATHAN   A.M.? Does that mean you're a morning person?

ROSENTHAL   What?

NATHAN   A morning...Never mind. What do you do, sir?

ROSENTHAL   I'm a columnist with *The New York Times*.

NATHAN   Very good.

ROSENTHAL   I used to edit *The New York Times*.

NATHAN   Alright, and you've got a thing or two to say
               about the Hebron Massacre.

ROSENTHAL   Damned right I do.

NATHAN   Alright, and the title of your speech?

ROSENTHAL   It's called "The Worth of Israel."

NATHAN   "The Worth."

ROSENTHAL   "The Worth of Israel."

NATHAN   Very good. You heard the rules?

ROSENTHAL   Uh? Yeah, I heard.

NATHAN   Alright, then, A.M. Rosenthal of *The New York
               Times*, you've got thirty seconds, starting...now.

ROSENTHAL   (*taking his time*) Baruch Goldstein committed a
               monstrous act of terrorism that cannot be softened
               by talk of his rage. But Israelis denounced the
               crime; some even saw it as a time for national
               contrition. After the massacre, the President of
               Israel went to Hebron to bow his head. And now,
               it is healthy and wise to ask some questions.
               When Pan Am 103 was bombed out of the sky,
               did Arab states immediately begin an
               investigation?

               Whistling bomb.

NATHAN   Wrap it up, please.

ROSENTHAL   When 22 Jews in an Istanbul synagogue were
murdered at prayer—

                    Explosion.

ROSENTHAL   Damn.

NATHAN   I'm sorry, Mr. Rosenthal. Would our last speaker
step up to the mike. Your name?

OZICK   Cynthia Ozick.

NATHAN   And you are?

OZICK   A writer and critic. I mainly work in prose, but
right now I'm working on a play.

NATHAN   A play.

OZICK   Yes.

NATHAN   Can you tell us a bit about it?

OZICK   Well, it's about denial of the Holocaust.

NATHAN   Very good, very good. Oughta do well for you.
You can't really go wrong with the Holocaust.
There's no business like Shoah business. Isn't
that right, Mr. Spielberg?

SPIELBERG   I'd like to thank the Academy for this award. It
means a lot to me, I owe so many thanks to so
many people, but there's one man in particular
without whom this picture could never have been
made.

NATHAN   Hitler. Alright, where were we?

OZICK   Over here, tatala.

NATHAN   Alright, Ms Ozick, and what is the name of your
speech?

OZICK   "Mutual Sorrow, Mutual Gain."

NATHAN

"Mutual Sorrow, Mutual Gain," very nice, very nice. Alright, then, Cynthia Ozick, writer, critic and, what the hell, playwright, you have thirty seconds to talk about the Hebron Massacre, starting...now.

OZICK

(*very quickly*) Always and always, the deaths of Jews and Arabs are paired. To pair murders is to count heads, and to count heads is to quantify killing, and to quantify killing is to denigrate the sacred meaning of a single human life. The idea of "extremists on both sides" leads to that tired old sleight-of-hand known as moral equivalence. Suddenly the mathematics of atrocity is back in place. Here is a massacre, by a Jew, of Arabs. Here are the murders, by Arabs, of Jewish employers, a Jewish father and son in Hebron, a pregnant Jewish housewife. If there is to be an equality of blame—

Whistling bomb.

NATHAN

Five seconds.

OZICK

—shouldn't there also be an equality of contrition? Consider the power of contrition alone, as a primary assertion of effective leadership.

Explosion.

OZICK

I mean the political power of sorrow, shame and grief.

NATHAN

Ms Ozick...

OZICK

What needs to be paired are not criminal acts of murder—

NATHAN

Ms Ozick, I'm afraid your time...

OZICK

—shut up—

NATHAN

You've exceeded your—

OZICK   …but demonstrations of contrition. Mutual
                contrition is above all a political act, and it is the
                right way back.

NATHAN   Alright, Ms Ozick. You went far past your alloted
                time, and so we're going to have to allow for
                rebuttal. Would anyone in the audience care to
                rebut Ms Ozick's position? Anyone at all? Just
                step right up.

STERNBERG   Yes, I have something to say.

NATHAN   Your name, sir?

STERNBERG   Rabbi Shlomo Sternberg, from Cambridge,
                Massachusets.

NATHAN   Can you say that five times fast.

                He starts. NATHAN interrupts.

                Rabbi…Rabbi…Tawk to me.

STERNBERG   What Ms Ozick refuses to confront is our shared
                responsibility — hers and mine — in these
                atrocities. Baruch Goldstein received his education
                from within the "modern orthodox" community.
                From all accounts, Dr. Goldstein was a paragon of
                self-sacrifice and devotion to others. It is hard to
                believe that such a person could become a mass
                murderer. It must take years of training. Dr.
                Goldstein was a model student at the Yeshiva of
                Flatbush, Yeshiva University and Einstein
                Medical School. I have yet to hear public
                statements of contrition from the leaders of these
                educational institutions.

NATHAN   Anyone else?

ELIACH   I'd like to respond to Rabbi Sternberg's rebuttal.

NATHAN   And you are?

ELIACH   Dr. Sarah Eliach, from Brooklyn.

NATHAN   Make it sing.

ELIACH   Rabbi Sternberg asks for a public statement of
                    contrition from Baruch Goldstein's former teachers
                    and principals. While we all deplore and condemn
                    the senseless murder of innocent individuals, we
                    cannot comply with his request for acquiesence in
                    his libel of Orthodox Jewish education.

EXCITED MAN   Rabbi Sternberg surely knows that there is no line
                    that goes from Orthodox Jewish education to
                    Hebron. Some of our alumni who move to Israel
                    live in Judea. Others have a different political
                    position. They all received the same education that
                    Baruch Goldstein did.

                        *NATHAN has had enough. He cuts off the
                        music and kicks everyone out. He finds the
                        piece of paper containing the BOSS'
                        telephone number. Calls her.*

Torture

NATHAN and the BOSS, at her place.

NATHAN

I don't speak Hebrew. Don't read it, neither. Neither do I read it. Used to, though. Used to be able to read Hebrew. Like, when I was thirteen.

NATHAN AT 13

(*singing*) Ma nish-ta-naw ha-lai-law ha-zeh mee-kawl ha-lay-lot? Mee-kawl ha-lay-lot?

THE RELATIVES

(*applauding*) Awwwwwwww!
Good singing, Nathan!
He's so cute!

NATHAN

I was the youngest, so I asked the four questions. Why is this night different than all other nights?

MOM

Ask the first question, Nathan.

NATHAN AT 13

She-b'chawl ha-lay-los aw-nu o-ch'leen chaw-maytz u-ma-tzaw, ha-lai-law ha-zeh ku-lo ma-tzaw?

NATHAN

When my Zaydie led the ceremony, it seemed to go on forever.

ZAYDIE, BUBBIE and NATHAN at 13 at the seder. ZAYDIE wears a hat.

You could smell the chicken soup simmering in my bubbie's kitchen. The kids would giggle and jostle. My zaydie took the ceremony very seriously. He wore a hat, not a yarmalke, and he stood as he recited the prayers. In Hebrew.

ZAYDIE

(*chanting*) Haw lach-maw an-yaw dee-a-chaw-lu a-vaw-haw-saw-naw b'ar-aw...

NATHAN	We did the entire Haggadah, including the songs.
THE OTHERS	(*robustly*) Di-di-ay-nu, di-di-ay-nu, di-di-ay-nu, dianu dianu!
NATHAN	When Zaydie died, Dad took over the ceremony. He made a few changes.
	ZAYDIE turns into DAD, BUBBIE into MOM.
DAD	Listen to this, Nathan. It says here, "Now we are slaves in a foreign land; next year may we be free in Jerusalem."
NATHAN	Right...
DAD	*I'm* not a slave. That's number one. Second, I don't want to go to Jerusalem. What are they, nuts? And get my head blown off?
NATHAN	So when he got to that bit:
DAD	Now we live in a free land; next year, may all those who want to go to Jerusalem, *go.*
NATHAN	As the years went by, he got bored.
DAD	This year, I'm going for a new record. Ready?
NATHAN	Ready...and...*now...*
DAD	(*very quickly*) BlessedartthouOeternalourGodKingofthe UniverseCreatorofthefruitofthevine.
NATHAN	Three seconds.
DAD	Drink the first glass of wine.
NATHAN	We went from reading the whole book, singing the songs, the whole bit.
ALL	(*trying to find the words*) Di...di...aynu?

MOM	I'll get the fish.
NATHAN	We got it down to a couple of blessings and a token reading of the story of how the Jews escaped from Yul Brynner. Oh, and the spilling of the drops of wine, to represent each of the ten plagues:
DAD	Blood.
THE OTHERS	Blood.
DAD	Frogs.
THE OTHERS	Frogs.
DAD	Vermin.
THE OTHERS	Vermin.
DAD	Aunty Yetta.
THE OTHERS	Aunty Ye—
NATHAN	Passover went from something meaningful in a language I didn't understand, to something meaningless in a language I did. Then my dad died. Now it's my turn to lead the seder.

> *They begin to make love, a young Palestinian boy appears:*

MOURAD	From the moment I was arrested, they put me in an atmosphere of fear and violence. Five to ten of them invaded my house smashing furniture, pictures and personal things They kidnapped me from my bed. and started beating me even before they asked me my name. They put me in an isolated cell where they covered my head with a hood that had been soaked in urine. They told me to lie on my back and with my hands tied

they hit
and kicked my testicles
Twice they strangled me
for up to a minute at a time,
beat me on the head
with a metal bar covered with rubber
They tied me to a stool
and with my head and legs on either side
beat me on the stomach
After this
they took me to be in the *shaba*
a long dark thin closed cupboard
where I was left
half conscious.
This continued for a month
during which time
I was not allowed to shower
or change my clothes
They arrested my aunt
who brought me up.
They know that I love her very much.
They told me they had to arrest her
because I would not confess.
They lifted me up
so I could see her
through a small window.
They told me my father was so sick
that I could not see him.
I was sentenced
to thirty months
for throwing stones.
The judge recognized
that this was to prevent the violence
they said
I would commit
against Israel.
This trial took place
when I was thirteen.

Morning

The next morning. NATHAN is reading the paper.

BOSS   Nathan?

NATHAN   Asshole.

BOSS   What?

NATHAN   Morning.

BOSS   Whatcha doing?

NATHAN   Reading.

BOSS   Uh?

NATHAN   *The New York Times*.

BOSS   It's Sunday? It isn't Sunday.

NATHAN   No.

BOSS   It can't be Sunday. I'm going to shul.

NATHAN   It's Saturday.

BOSS   You read *The New York Times* on Saturday?

NATHAN   I read it every day.

BOSS   Why?

NATHAN   I like to start my morning with the Big Lies. It makes the little ones a little more palatable.

BOSS   Lies, like what?

NATHAN	Like A.M. Rosenthal. He writes an entire column about Hebron, making sure to mention the 1929 massacre of Jews by Arabs, totally ignoring Goldstein's massacre. It doesn't exist, because it gets in the way of his theory, which is that the poor 400 Jews who squatted in Hebron need to be protected from the 100,000 Palestinian terrorists who have the temerity to live their squalid lives there.
BOSS	Don't you think they need to be protected?
NATHAN	Is that coffee I smell?
BOSS	You sure you don't want to come to shul?
NATHAN	I'm sure.
BOSS	I got box seats. Going once...going twice...
NATHAN	Why do you go?
BOSS	...Because it's there.
NATHAN	You feel anything for it?
BOSS	I love the music.
NATHAN	Right.
BOSS	It's important. I don't want to lose touch with who I am.
NATHAN	You mean, with who you were.
BOSS	No. Who I am.
NATHAN	And who's that?
BOSS	It's a litte early to play Who Am I, okay?
NATHAN	Okay....You donate money to Israel?
BOSS	What?

NATHAN   Do you—donate—

BOSS   Yeah.

NATHAN   "Yeah."

BOSS   What's wrong with that?

NATHAN   Nothing. If you want to support murder and
                oppression.

BOSS   Oh puh-leez. What, did you wake up with your
                morals in a knot? "Support murder and"…I am
                supporting schools, hospitals…

NATHAN   Border closings.

BOSS   Border cl—Look. You don't know what you're—
                don't accuse me of "oppressing" anyone. I don't
                want to talk about this anymore, okay?

NATHAN   Okay.

BOSS   Thank you.

NATHAN   The thing is.

BOSS   Oh Jesus.

NATHAN   You send money to Israel. They use that money to
                build settlements. Some crazy fuck comes along
                with a machine gun, mows down a buncha dirty
                Arabs. It doesn't just happen. He shouldn't'a been
                there in the first place. Why is he there? Because
                of your money. Our money.

BOSS   Uh huh. It's funny, isn't it, how everything we do
                is wrong.

NATHAN   I'm not saying that.

BOSS   No, no. You, you spend all your time reading
                about Isr—kvetching about Israel, and what it is
                to be Jewish, and and…What is wrong with you?
                You have no idea. How lucky you are. How lucky

	all of us are, to have Israel. For 2,000 years, Nathan, we were persecuted.
NATHAN	And now it's time to return the favour?
BOSS	Nathan, you can't. Listen. I want to tell you something. Because I don't think you understand. The first time I went to Israel, I went to the Holocaust Memorial. Yad Vashem. You know?
NATHAN	Yeah.
BOSS	I mean nothing can prepare you for that, Nathan. To see those pictures. Especially of the children. What they did to the children. How they suffered. Um. One of the photos was of a little boy, with his arms up and...he um, had this hat, this uh, he was wearing this hat...they shot him because of who he was. When I saw that picture, Nathan, I knew that we need this country. And I am sorry for the Palestinian people, truly I am. But there is nothing I will say, not a word will I say, against this country. Can you understand that?
NATHAN	Yes. Because you love Israel.
BOSS	I do. I feel it.
NATHAN	People like you scare the shit outta me. You stand there and use those children to justify what we've done to the Palestinians. How can you do that?
BOSS	Fuk you.
NATHAN	Gezundheit.
BOSS	You accuse me of...you're saying that because I want to make sure that what happened to us never happens again, that I'm worse than Baruch Goldstein? Is that what you're telling me? I don't believe that. You read it somewhere. It sounded good so you added it to your armour. It doesn't mean a fucking thing, none of it, because you don't believe it. What do you believe?

NATHAN	I believe…you're late for shul.

EX-WIFE appears.

BOSS	Why are you doing this?
NATHAN	What?
EX-WIFE	Pushing me away.
NATHAN	I don't want you should be late.
BOSS	Answer the fucking question.
NATHAN	I vant to be a loner.
EX-WIFE	Good. Then get out.
NATHAN	Get out?
EX-WIFE	I packed your suitcase. Go on.
NATHAN	I don't want to go.
EX-WIFE	Fine. Then I will.
NATHAN	Just stay a minute.
BOSS	I can't. I'm late. (*starts to go*) Would you do me a favour?
NATHAN	Walk your dog?
BOSS	I don't have a dog.
NATHAN	Then yes.
BOSS	Would you hold me?
NATHAN	Hold you.
EX-WIFE	You know what that is?
NATHAN	Uh huh.

EX-WIFE	Then?
NATHAN	I don't think so.
BOSS	What?
NATHAN	I said I don't think so.
BOSS	You prick. You talk about compassion for people halfway around the world,
EX-WIFE	and you can't even give it to someone halfway across the room.
BOSS	You know what? I didn't want it. I was testing you.
NATHAN	I knew that. I detected the insincerity.
BOSS	Why did you come here?
NATHAN	Hm?
BOSS	Are you listening to me?
NATHAN	No.
BOSS	Why did you sleep with me?
NATHAN	You asked me to.
BOSS	You didn't want to?
NATHAN	Not especially. To tell you the truth, you digust me. I can't stand the smell of you. I want to take a shower. I wish I could chop off my fingers, my tongue, my dick. I'll probably die of some disease you gave me.
BOSS	Are you listening to me?
NATHAN	Yes.
BOSS	Why did you sleep with me?

NATHAN	I wanted to be with you.
BOSS	Do you still want to be with me?
NATHAN	Yes. I'm sorry.
EW-WIFE	Are you?
NATHAN	No.
BOSS	Christ.
NATHAN	I mean yes.
EW-WIFE	I think you should go.
NATHAN	That is to say.
BOSS	Will you go please?
NATHAN	Uh.
EX-WIFE	Will you go?
NATHAN	Um. Er. Uh.
BOSS	Get out of my house.

He leaves, taking his paper with him.

The Seder

NATHAN returns to his apartment. He pours a cup of wine, holds it up.

NATHAN

Blessed art thou, O Lord our God, Ruler of the Universe, Creator of the fruit of the vine.

Pause.

Amen.

Drinks.

On February 25th, 1994, Dr. Baruch Goldstein, a settler from Kiryat Arba, committed a...

He shoves the books off his desk in one motion; takes a moment to recover.

massacre at the Tomb of the Patriarchs in Hebron.

The Government of Israel decided to appoint a Commission of Inquiry to determine whether Goldstein acted alone or with accomplices,

(*Words in Haggadah*) Blessed art thou, O Lord our God, Ruler of the Universe, Who has chosen us from all peoples, and exalted us above all nations—

The telephone rings.

NATHAN

Hello?

MOM

Hello, darling.

NATHAN

Hi, Mom.

MOM

How you doing?

NATHAN	Same as yesterday when you called.
MOM	So: you were gonna let me know about the boys?
NATHAN	I was?
MOM	Are you bringing them to the seder?
NATHAN	No.
MOM	Oi. I'm worried about you.
NATHAN	That's odd.
MOM	The first year without Pat and the boys.
NATHAN	I'm fine.
MOM	I just—
NATHAN	I'm fine.
MOM	I—
NATHAN	*I'm.* Fine.
MOM	Fine. So goodbye.
NATHAN	Goodbye.

> *They hang up.*

NATHAN   (*returning to his seder*) Blessed art thou O Lord our God Ruler of the Universe Creator of the fruit of the vine.

Amen.

Blessed art thou O Lord our God Ruler of the Universe, who has chosen us from all peoples, and exalted us above all nations, and sanctified us with—

> *The telephone rings.*

NATHAN	Hello?
EX-WIFE	It's me. Your ex-wife.
NATHAN	Yes?
EX-WIFE	Did Ben take his medicine?
NATHAN	(*cartoon voice*) Yes, dear.
EX-WIFE	You forgot to give it to him last time.
NATHAN	(*cartoon voice*) Yes, dear.
EX-WIFE	Did you give it to him?
NATHAN	(*cartoon voice*) Yes, dear.
EX-WIFE	Such an asshole.

They hang up.

NATHAN	Blessed art thou O Lord our God Ruler of the—
ZAYDIE	(*appears*) This is your seder?
NATHAN	Zaydie?
ZAYDIE	Where are the boys?
NATHAN	Sleeping.
ZAYDIE	What happened to the seder? Where is the family?
NATHAN	I don't have an answer to that.
ZAYDIE	You could at least read in Hebrew, maybe?
NATHAN	Baruch ata adonai, elohaynu melech haolum. Baruch ata adonai... Barucha Goldstein adonai... Baruch Goldstein got annoyed... Baruch Goldstein shot some Arabs...

BEN runs out.

BEN	Bang!
NATHAN	Jesus!
BEN	Sorry Daddy.
NATHAN	You know you're not supposed to play with guns.
BEN	It's not a gun, it's my finger.
NATHAN	What are you doing out of bed?
BEN	I'm not tired. Can you tell me a story?
NATHAN	No. I'm not telling you another story.
BEN	FINE! THEN I WON'T BE YOUR FRIEND!
NATHAN	Lower your voice. I don't want you waking up your brother.
BEN	He's dead.
NATHAN	Pardon me?
BEN	We were playing Arabs and Jews and he's an Arab and I shot him.
NATHAN	"Arabs" and "Jews". Where did you learn about "Arabs" and "Jews"?
BEN	From Mummy. She told me you were Jewish.
NATHAN	Uh huh. What did she tell you?
BEN	That the Arabs are bad guys and they want to kill the Jews.
NATHAN	It's a little more complicated than that.
BEN	Tell me, Daddy.
NATHAN	It's time for bed.
BEN	Nooooo, tell me.

NATHAN   Well. Alright, let's say some people came in here and said, "This is our house. You have to leave."

BEN   But it's our house.

NATHAN   But what if they said it was their house a long time ago.

BEN   But...

NATHAN   What would you do? How would you get your house back?

Beat.

BEN   Bang!

NATHAN   Exactly. Alright. Bedtime.

BEN goes off. NATHAN returns to the seder, realizes he needs something, goes off. Mossad agents come in, rearrange things on the desk, creating a more traditional looking seder table; then, they hide under the desk.

NATHAN brings back a box of crackers. He's wearing his grandfather's hat.

NATHAN   Drink the first cup of wine.

He drinks it.

Blessed art thou, O Lord our God, Ruler of the Universe, Creator of the Fruit of the Loom.

He takes out a cracker.

This matzah we eat.

He breaks half of it.

NATHAN   Nobody look. Nobody look. I'm hiding the afikoman. Hiding the afikoman.

This is the bread of affliction which our ancestors ate in the land of Egypt. All who are hungry — let them come and eat. All who are needy let them come and celebrate the Passover with us.

> *ZAYDIE comes out from under the table. They look at each other. NATHAN gives him his hat.*

ZAYDIE
The Torah tells of four sons. One who is wise, and one is contrary; one who is simple and one who does not even know how to ask a question.

> *ASHWARI appears.*

Who's here already?

NATHAN
Sorry. Hanan Ashwari, my grandfather.

ASHWARI
I am honoured to meet you.

ZAYDIE
Mm hm.

NATHAN
And this is Noam Chomsky, professor of linguistics at MIT.

CHOMSKY
Good Pesach.

ZAYDIE
A nice Jewish boy.

NATHAN
Wait'll he talks about Israel.

JANE
Hi, I'm Jane.

ZAYDIE
Mm hm. "Jane," this is a name for a Jewish girl?

JANE
I'm not Jewish, but I love the Jewish people. When I was a little girl, I wanted to be Jewish so badly. You people are so persecuted? I remember reading The Diary of Anne Frank and thinking, I wish *I* was Jewish.

> *Pause; the five are now gathered round the seder table.*

ZAYDIE	The wise son asks, What is the meaning of the laws and customs which the Lord our God has commanded us? To him you shall explain all the laws of the Passover, to the very last detail of the afikoman. Did you hide the afikoman?
NATHAN	Yes, I did. And I've written the answer to the Middle East question on the afikoman, so whoever finds it gets an extra special treat.
JANE	I was at a seder once, and *I* found the afikoman. Me!

Pause.

ZAYDIE	The contrary son asks:
NATHAN	Zaydie.
ZAYDIE	Be quiet, I'm talking.
NATHAN	I know that, but...
ZAYDIE	The *contrary* son asks...
NATHAN	You jumped ahead. We didn't ask the four questions.
ZAYDIE	So? You didn't light the candles either.
JANE	I brought candles! Hanan, would you help me do the blessing?
ASHWARI	I don't know it.
JANE	You read Hebrew, don't you?
ASHWARI	Of course.
JANE	I'll start; you follow.

They light the candles; NATHAN finds himself deeply moved by the traditional singing of the blessing.

ZAYDIE   That brings us to the Four Questions.

NATHAN   Zaydie. It's my turn to lead the seder.

                After a moment, ZAYDIE passes his hat to
                NATHAN, who puts it on and begins:

NATHAN   Now it is written, I don't know where exactly it is
                written but it must be written somewhere, that it
                is our duty to retell the story of the Exodus. Why?
                So that we, the Jews, the Chosen Ones, the the
                the...

JANE   A Light Unto...

NATHAN   A Light Unto Nations, thank you Jane, A Light
                Unto Nations, so that we can recall what was done
                for us in our time of *need.* Thus we read of our
                oppression, and our deliverance. *Yet* we do not
                see. That we have become the oppressors. How
                has this happened? Let us ask some new
                questions, pertinent questions....How is this
                country—Israel—different than all other countries?
                Noam Chomsky.

NOAM   I'm sorry?

NATHAN   Listen up, Noam. How is this country diff—

NOAM   Yes. I uh, I heard the question. I thought I told
                you once but, uhh alright. Israel is different
                because no other country is permitted to commit
                such terrible rights abuses and at the same time is
                revered as a paragon of moral rectitude.

NATHAN   Thank you.

NOAM   Much to its own detriment.

NATHAN   Right.

NOAM   I thought we'd covered this.

NATHAN   Now, how did the early Zionists rationalize the creation of a Jewish state in Palestine? Hanan Ashwari.

ASHWARI   Yes?

NATHAN   The Answer.

ASHWARI   Yes, alright. By claiming that no one lived there. *You* know, as in the slogan, "A country without a people for a people without a country."

NATHAN   Right. And that is despite the fact that it had been inhabited for—

ASHWARI   Yes.

NATHAN   Centuries.

ASHWARI   Clearly.

NATHAN   Good. Alright. I think we're getting somewhere. Um. How did the inhabitants of Palestine react to massive Jewish immigration? Jane.

JANE   They resisted.

NATHAN   Would you care to elaborate?

JANE   Again?

NATHAN   I don't follow.

JANE   Apparently not.

NATHAN   Okay. Professor Said, if and when you are invited to speak to Jewish audiences, what will you tell them about the future of Jews in Palestine?

        Pause.

        Professor Said...future...of the Jews...in Palestine.

SAID   I have already answered this question.

NATHAN	You have.
SAID	In the library. Look, Nathan. We've been through all this. Now look. What exactly what do you want?
NATHAN	I j— I have some questions.
CHOMSKY	You've already asked them.
JANE	Besides, you're not really listening to the answers.
NATHAN	Of course I am.
SAID	Why did you invite us? To share your ceremony?
CHOMSKY	What do you want from us?
ASHWARI	You fall in love with an idea the way you fall in love with a woman.
SAID	And when our ideas are no longer attractive…
ASHWARI	You will push us away.
NATHAN	I'm asking questions.
SAID	The wrong questions.
NATHAN	The same questions you ask.
ASHWARI	Precisely. But they are not your questions.
JANE	You think you are the wise son.
CHOMSKY	In what way wise?
JANE	You think you are the contrary son.
SAID	Contrary to what?
JANE	You think you are the simple son.
ASHWARI	It is not so simple.

JANE

In fact, you are the son who does not even know
how to ask a question.

*A huge explosion; all hell breaks loose...two
HASIDIM - right out of Vaudeville - appear:*

1ST HASID

Don't step there!

NATHAN

Where?

1ST HASID

What's the matter with you? That's somebody's skin.

NATHAN

Where?

2ND HASID

Under your foot. Move.

*NATHAN moves. 2ND HASID scrapes the
skin up, puts it in a bag.*

NATHAN

Where am I?

1ST HASID

Jerusalem. Hamas blew up another bus today.
We're collecting the blood and skin and brains of
the innocent.

2ND HASID

No one can be buried unless they are whole.

1ST HASID

That way, comes Moshiach, they'll be holy.

2ND HASID

You slay me, Hershel.

1ST HASID

Never mind. Hold this,

*1ST HASID hands 2ND HASID the bag;
scrapes something up; puts it in the bag.*

2ND HASID

Is that a finger or a...

1ST HASID

Oi!

2ND HASID

That's what I thought.

1ST HASID

I got news for you.

2ND HASID

What's that?

1ST HASID	It's not even kosher.
2ND HASID	Oi! It must be Nathan's!

The telephone rings.

NATHAN	Hello?
CONSPIRATOR	Did you do it?
NATHAN	Do what?
CONSPIRATOR	Kill Netanyahu?
NATHAN	Look…
CONSPIRATOR	What are you waiting for? There's gonna be a civil war. You have to do something. Forget about the massacre already. It's done, it's over; you think the Jews and Arabs are waiting for a history lesson? Don't get stuck on Hebron. You gotta move with the times. Move! Move! Move!

The telephone rings.

NATHAN	Hello?
MOM	Nathan, did you hear?
NATHAN	Hear what?
MOM	They shot Rabin.
NATHAN	Who did?
MOM	At a peace rally. They shot him.
NATHAN	Is he dead?
MOM	No. They took him to the hospital. They say it was a Jew. A Jew!

He hangs up. Orthodox Jews enter, dancing and singing.

SETTLER 1	Hero of Israel! Hero of Israel! There should be more like him!
SETTLER 2	(*his head covered in a white shawl*) This is the tallis of Goldstein! Put it on! It is like touching the saint.
NATHAN	Saint!
SETTLER 3	He is a saint! He has saved us! We came here to salute this righteous man.
NATHAN	He killed 29 men at prayer!
SETTLER 4	It says in the Torah that with those who want to kill you, you must kill them first.
NATHAN	Listen…there are only 450 of you here, and a hundred thousand Palestinians. You have to move somewhere else.
SETTLER 2	Our return to Hebron is not open for discussion. If Hebron falls, Jerusalem falls.
SETTLER 4	This is the most perfidious government that ever existed.
ALL	Death to Rabin! Death to Rabin! Death to Rabin!
	The telephone rings.
NATHAN	Hello?
MOM	Nathan, did you hear what happened in Hebron?
NATHAN	What?
MOM	The Jewish underground murdered three students at the Islamic College.
	He hangs up.
SETTLER	You don't "understand" Hebron.
NATHAN	I'm trying to.

SETTLER	You never will. Listen. The Arabs think it's theirs; it's ours. We got there first. Abraham bought it. Abraham, our father.
NATHAN	The Arabs call Abraham father too.
SETTLER	You are a Jew. And you are either with us or against us. If you choose to go with the Arab, you will be against your own people. Do you think the Arabs will take you in? No! Once they have used you, *used you to get what they want,* they will throw you into the sea.

The telephone rings.

NATHAN	Hello?
MOM	Nathan, are you watching?
NATHAN	What?
MOM	Rabin's funeral. His granddaughter's doing the eulogy. You should listen.

NOA, Rabin's granddaughter, enters.

NOA	Forgive me if I do not want to talk about peace. I want to talk about my grandfather. You always awake from a nightmare, but since yesterday I only awake into a nightmare — the nightmare of life without you, and that is impossible to fathom.
NATHAN	Noa Ben Artzi-Pelosoff?
NOA	Yes?
NATHAN	My name's Nathan Abramowitz.
NOA	Yes?
NATHAN	I understand you're writing a book about your grandfather.
NOA	Yes.

NATHAN   I hear you're getting a million dollars.

NOA   That's right.

NATHAN   I'd love to get a look at it.

NOA   On the ground, pig!

                She starts to make love to him.

NATHAN   Oh my God. Yes. Noa. Yes.

NOA   Come on, Nathan. Live in the moment, just like
                we do in Israel.

NATHAN   I'm living, I'm living.

NOA   You want to touch my gun? I'm in the army you
                know.

NATHAN   Yes, your gun, your gun.

NOA   You like this?

NATHAN   Uh huh.

NOA   What about that?

NATHAN   You read my mind. Tell me, what do you think of
                the peace process?

NOA   I think it's very good

NATHAN   Uh huh?

NOA   I want to say to the Arabs, we want peace with
                you. But if you so much as think about invading
                us again, we will destroy you as surely as we
                annihilated the Amalekites.

NATHAN   Okay, that's clear. What do you think about a pull
                out?

NOA   No! Don't stop, don't stop.

NATHAN	Oh God. Do the eulogy.
NOA	What?
NATHAN	The eulogy, the eulogy.
NOA	You sick bastard, I want to fuck you all night.
NATHAN	Do it!
NOA	Grandfather, you were and still are our hero.
NATHAN	Oh yes, oh yes.
NOA	I wanted you to know…
NATHAN	Mm…
NOA	…that everytime I did anything…
NATHAN	Yeah, yeah.
NOA	I saw you in front of me.
RABIN/ZAYDIE	Stop this!
NATHAN	Zaydie?
NOA	Grandfather!
RABIN/ZAYDIE	You ought to be ashamed of yourself!
NOA	Pull out! Pull out!

The telephone rings.

CONSUL	You defile the memory of the dead.
NATHAN	Not true.
CONSUL	Did you weep at the funeral of Rabin?
NATHAN	No.
CONSUL	You see!

NATHAN	But I wanted to.
CONSUL	Liar.
NATHAN	It's true.
CONSUL	Then why didn't you?
NATHAN	I felt manipulated.
CONSUL	By the death of a man of peace?
NATHAN	Peace! He ordered the bombing of Lebanon!
CONSUL	He shook the hand of his enemy! He was a Jew. And you didn't weep?
NATHAN	I wanted to.
CONSUL	Then weep!

He hangs up.

NATHAN	Spill a drop of wine for each of the ten plagues. Blood.

Pause.

JANE	At the library, you asked me:
SAID	Why is this massacre different.
NATHAN	Frog·?
JANE	You felt revulsion.
SAID	Disgust.
ASHWARI	Pity for the victims.
CHOMSKY	Revulsion that one of your own.
JANE	That a Jew.
ASHWARI	That an Israeli would do such a thing.

NATHAN   Lice.

SAID   When you heard that Goldstein had been beaten to death.

CHOMSKY   Beaten to death by the Palestinians.

JANE   You felt horror, too.

SAID   At the death of Goldstein.

CHOMSKY   Because his life means more.

ASHWARI   Than the life of an Arab.

SAID   Of 29 Arabs.

NATHAN   Wild beasts.

SAID   "It was Purim after all."

JANE   "The answer was perfectly clear."

ASHWARI   "Thank God it all ended well."

CHOMSKY   "The natural situation."

NATHAN   Pestlience. Boils.

SAID   You want to help us?

ASHWARI   You want us to have a state?

NATHAN   I.

JANE   Yes?

NATHAN   Well. I.

SAID   Yes, Nathan?

NATHAN   Hail. Locusts.

SAID   You're running out of plagues, Nathan.

ASHWARI	The Arab is a murderous thief.
SAID	"You cannot trust the Arab."
CHOMSKY	"Even when he appears to be civilized."
SAID	The plane went down.
ASHWARI	Arab terrorists.
CHOMSKY	Or perhaps mechanical failure.
SAID	Arabs is better.
JANE	The building blew up.
ASHWARI	Arabs.
CHOMSKY	Or perhaps the militia.
JANE	Arab terrorists.
ASHWARI	Cockroaches.
SAID	Exterminate them.
CHOMSKY	Erase them from history.
NATHAN	Darkness.
ASHWARI	We don't exist.
NATHAN	Slaying of the first born.
SAID	You have run out of plagues.
ASHWARI	Ask your questions, Nathan.

The telephone rings.

NATHAN	Hello?
MOM	Hello, darling.
NATHAN	Hello, Mother.

MOM	What's doing?
NATHAN	Nothing.
MOM	Good Pesach.
NATHAN	Same to you.
MOM	We're going to the Bernbaums.
NATHAN	Uh huh.
MOM	The Bernbaums. You remember. With the son.
NATHAN	Oh yeah.
MOM	So what are you doing?
NATHAN	Oh you know.
MOM	Did you hear what happened in Hebron?
NATHAN	No, what.
MOM	Abraham bought a cave.
NATHAN	That's nice.
MOM	So how's things with you?
NATHAN	Not bad. How were the Bernbaums last night?
MOM	Oh fine. We didn't eat 'til midnight.
NATHAN	Really.
MOM	Their son made such a fuss.
NATHAN	Uh huh.
MOM	Did you hear what happened in Hebron?
NATHAN	No, what.
MOM	The Arabs built a mosque over the cave.

NATHAN	Really.
MOM	So, what's with you?
NATHAN	Oh, not much.
MOM	How are the boys?
NATHAN	Fine.
MOM	When's the graduation ceremony?
NATHAN	End of the month.
MOM	I can't wait. Did you hear what happened in Hebron?
NATHAN	No, what?
MOM	Some crazy settler murdered 29 Arabs.
NATHAN	Really.
MOM	It's crazy. And how are you?
NATHAN	Oh fine.
MOM	Mrs. Bernbaum died.
NATHAN	Oh well.
MOM	How are the boys?
NATHAN	Dimmwd.
MOM	What a shame. Did you hear what happened in Hebron?
NATHAN	No, what?…What happened?…Mom?…Mom?

He hangs up.

NATHAN   My questions.

Did I help Baruch Goldstein murder 29 Palestinians?

Am I at the side of Baruch Goldstein?

Am I Baruch Goldstein?

Do I believe, I mean really believe, that Jews have a greater right to live than do Palestinians?

Do I believe, against all my best instincts and hopes and understanding of the way the world works, that my life is more valuable than the life of a Palestinian? Of an Arab? A filthy Arab?

The guests start to pack up.

A terrorist who would stab me in the back the first chance he got? A Jew hating, smelly, hummous eating—. Wait. Um. No. Those aren't the questions.

What am I doing?

The others are ready to go.

Don't go. Those aren't the questions. Find the afikoman.

There is a knock at the door.

Come on, Hanan, *look* for the matzah.

The knocking continues.

Jane, find the matzah…What happened to the seder?…Keep looking.

Loud knocking.

NATHAN   Yes? Who is it?

NATHAN opens the door; a young boy stands there.

NATHAN   Are you hungry?... "All who are hungry. All who are needy." Well, that's pretty much all of us, isn't it? Come in. ...Everyone, this is Baruch Goldstein...He's 13 years old...A student at the Yeshiva of Flatbush in Brooklyn, New York. Come in. He wants to say something to us. Come in...come in...alright, Benjy...go ahead...

                The others are sitting at the dismantled seder table; GOLDSTEIN addresses the audience; we had NATHAN wrap him in the tallis which the settlers brought in

BARUCH   Protest Against War

                War is a threatening and fearful thing
                with murder,
                killing,
                shedding of blood,
                cruelty
                and a burden to the wounded.

                War causes much distress for the country,
                soldiers
                and their families.

                Many people die in war
                and leave behind
                bereaved families,
                bereaved parents,
                young orphans,
                and a nation that,
                standing back,
                sees all that occured
                and is sad
                in its heart.

                Also,
                according to the Jewish religion,
                war is prohibited.

One of the important things in the Torah is
"do not murder"—
and in war
many people are murdered.

In the Torah
it is written
"do not covet."

War is caused, according to most,
from this—
that a country covets the land of another country
or its resources.

The Jewish nation always wants peace
and always wanted peace and,
in prayers,
one says that God will make peace
over all of Israel
and there will be no war in the land.

Who will give something
to bring about
a situation such as this—
that all human beings will live in peace,
will not murder
and will not covet the land
of one's neighbour,
and peace will prevail in the entire world?

Who will give to bring this about?

NATHAN   I found it. I found it, Zaydie.

> *NATHAN goes to GOLDSTEIN; holds him*
> *in an embrace. GOLDSTEIN backs away,*
> *joins the others at the table, where they*
> *become the Judges of Israel.*

Judges 5

JUDGE 1

The witness
is a visitor
from Canada

NATHAN

I would like to thank
the commission
for allowing me
the opportunity to speak

JUDGE 4

You mentioned in your letter
that you felt concerned
about the implications of the massacre
for Jews outside of Israel

NATHAN

Yes
I followed the news reports
about the inquiry
and became convinced that you
the Judges of Israel
would find the courage
to tell the truth
about this massacre

JUDGE 4

The evidence in cl   Dr. Baruch Goldstein bears
direct responsibility for the massacre.

NATHAN

The massacre was not
merely the action of one
deranged man
but the inevitable
I might even say logical
consequence
of Israeli policy
toward the Palestinian people

JUDGE 1

Have you been to Israel
before

NATHAN

No
This is my first time

JUDGE 1

How long do you intend to stay

NATHAN

Long enough
to get a feeling
for the country

JUDGE 1

What does that mean

NATHAN

It means that
up until this moment
my only experience of Israel
has been a vicarious one
I suppose you could say that
for me
Israel is an abstract idea

JUDGE 1

An
Abstract idea

NATHAN

I love the Jewish people
and this country which
I have never seen
with my own eyes
I visit it through books
newspapers
television
and radio
and through the experiences
of friends and relatives
who have lived here
or visited
Israel is
my lover, my wife, my friend my
child
parent
grandparent and
teacher
I love you O Israel
I would never harm you
never wish to see harm done to you
nor
by you

I fear that
if the Jewish state
and the Jewish people
continue to act as we do
we will disappear as surely
as the Palestinian people
whose homes we have taken
whose families we have dispersed
whose dignity we have denied
whose dreams we have ended

JUDGE 1

Well
Mr. Abramowitz
may I say that
I have lived in Israel
my entire life
and that for me
and for my friends
and for my family
and for the people who live here
and who struggle daily with
these questions
that Israel
is not an abstraction
but a very real place
We appreciate your comments
and your observations
But they are of no concern
to those of us who live here

JUDGE 2

The evidence is clear. Dr. Baruch Goldstein bears
direct responsibility for the massacre because the
evidence unequivocally indicates that he carried it
out. All stages of the event, including his
preparations and behaviour on the morning of
February 25th, 1994, indicate that his actions were
premeditated.

JUDGE 1

We were asked to investigate the massacre and to
determine findings and draw conclusions regarding
the circumstances related to it.

JUDGE 4

We recommend, first and foremost, that
arrangements intended to create complete
separation between the Muslim and Jewish

	worshippers be adopted, in order to ensure the safety of all worshippers, and to prevent friction, disputes and acts of violence.
JUDGE 3	Separate entrance gates will be set aside for Muslim and Jewish worshippers. Members of one religion will not be permitted to enter into an area in which prayers of the other religion are taking place at that time.
JUDGE 2	The massacre at the Tomb of the Patriarchs in Hebron was a base and murderous act, in which innocent people bending in prayer to their maker were killed.
JUDGE 4	We presented the lessons which must be learned from this tragic incident so that, as far as possible, the repetition of criminal acts such as these can be prevented. We made a series of recommendations meant to assist in returning things to normal both in the Tomb of the Patriarchs in particular, and generally in Hebron.
JUDGE 1	Let us hope that our inquiry and our report will indeed contribute to that end.
NATHAN	Drink the last cup of wine Now we are slaves Next year may we be free.

He exits.

The End.

Sources

p11 *On February 25th...*from "Commission of Inquiry into the Massacre at the Tomb of the Patriarchs in Hebron, Excerpts from the Report," translated and printed by the Government Press Office, Jerusalem. p. 1.
p.12 *The witness...*the testimony was reconstructed from the "Commission of Inquiry" as well as newspaper accounts of the inquiry, chiefly *The New York Times* between March 9th, 1994 and April 7th, 1994.
p.42 *I was not surprised by it...* (paraphrase) from Said's essay "Further Reflections on the Hebron Massacre—March 1994" in his *Peace and Its Discontents* (Vintage, 1995), pp 53-54.

*Arabic literature is heavily censored...*paraphrase of various writings by Said. See "Embargoed Literature" p. 372, and "A Conversation With Salman Rushdie" p. 119 in *The Politics of Dispossession, The Struggle for Palestinian Self-Determination 1969-1994* (Pantheon, 1994)

*If and when you are invited...*and Said's answer are both from "A Conversation With Salman Rushdie" p.123.

I think the Israelis... from "Interview with Hanan Ashrawi" in *Tikkun,* March/April 1993, p.36.
p.43   *The reasons were personal...*from "Leibowitz on the Expulsions" in *Tikkun,* March/April 1993, p.42.
p.52   *This goes back to Ben-Gurion...*see Chomsky's *The Fateful Triangle* (Black Rose Books, 1984), especially the chapter "The Legacy of the Founding Fathers," p.52ff, quoting Ben-Gurion and, here, Meir: "It was not as though there was a Palestinian people in Palestine considering itself as a Palestinian people and we came and threw them out and took their country away from them They did not exist."
p.58   *I think of the terrible effect...*(paraphrase) from "Interview with Hanan Ashrawi" in *Tikkun,* March/April 1993, p.37.
p.60 *The murder of more than...* from "Disarm the West Bank Settlers," *The New York Times,* Feb. 26, 1994, op-ed.
p.61   *Baruch Goldstein committed...* from "The Worth of Israel," *The New York Times,* Mar. 1, 1994, op-ed.
p.62   *There's no business...*a joke told in Israel, related by David Mamet in an essay on the film "Schindler's List".

*Hitler...*remark by Daniel Brooks on hearing Spielberg's Academy Award acceptance speech (very loosely paraphrased) for best director for the film "Schindler's List".
p.63   *Always and always...*from "Mutual Sorrow, Mutual Gain," *The New York Times,* Mar. 2, 1994, op-ed.

p.64   *What Ms Ozick refuses to confront...*from letter to the editor by Rabbi Shlomo Sternberg, *The New York Times,* March 9, 1994.

Rabbi Sternberg asks for a public statement; and *Rabbi Sternberg surely knows* (p.65)...from letter to the editor by Rabbi David Eliach and Joel B. Wolowelsky, *The New York Times,* March 18, 1994.

p.66   *Ma nish-ta-naw...*and what follows are taken from *Passover Haggadah Revised Edtion,* Rabbi Nathan Goldberg, (Ktav Publishing House Inc., 1994). Translation: Why is this night different than all other nights? On all other nights we may eat either leavened or unleavened bread, but on this night, only unleavened bread.

*Haw lach-maw...*Translation: This is the bread of affliction which our ancestors ate in the land of Egypt.

p.67   *Di-di-ay-nu...*from the Haggadah; an upbeat song about how thankful we are for God's great works.

*Now we live in a free land...*from Cyril Sherman's revised Haggadah, circa 1980.

p.68   *From the moment I was arrested...*from a statement by Mourad Jadallah, a 17 year-old Palestinian, presented at a United Nations-sponsored conference on Palestine in Toronto in July, 1994, reprinted in *NOW* Magazine, June 30 - July 6, 1994.

p.77   *Blessed art thou...*this and all quotes that follow are from the Goldberg Haggadah. Nathan is reading selected passages.

p.84   *Israel is different because...*(paraphrase) from Chomsky's *The Fateful Triangle,* especially pp 5-6.

p.85   *a country without a people...*Chaim Weizmann, leader of the Zionist movement, in 1914; quoted in Ron David, "Arabs and Israel For Beginners (Writers & Readers, 1993), p. 94.

p.89   *Hero of Israel!...*the settlers' quotes are all taken from the article "Hundreds of Jews Gather To Honor Hebron Killer," *The New York Times,* April 1, 1994, p. A5.

p.90   *Forgive me if I do not want...*from Noa Ben Artzi-Pelosoff's eulogy for Yitzhak Rabin, widely reprinted, here from *The Globe & Mail,* Nov. 7, 1995, p.A21.

p.95   *You cannot trust the Arab...*(paraphrase) from an Israeli army booklet issued to soldiers during 1973 war, quoted by Edward Said in *The Question of Palestine,* p. 91.

p.99   *alright, Benjy...*Goldstein's original given name was Benjamin—his nickname was Benjy; like many Jews who moved to Israel, he adopted its Hebrew equivalent.

p.99   *Protest Against War...*by Benjamin Goldstein, age 13; reprinted in *The New York Times* under the headline "'Do Not Murder,'" March 9, 1994, p. A15.

p.103   *The evidence is clear...*this and the following are taken from "The Commission of Inquiry."

Glossary of Words and Phrases

There's a saying that if you put ten Jews in a room you get eleven opinions; the theory holds true for word pronunciation. Consult your local Rabbi or use your best judgment.

afikoman - a piece of matzah hidden before the Passover meal begins; the lucky child who finds it gets a reward, often monetary.

aliyah - the greatest thing a Jew can do, we are told, is "return" or "ascend" to the land of Israel; this is called making aliyah. The second best thing a Jew can do is marry another Jew; this is called making your mother happy.

Amalekites - bad guys in the Old Testament, wiped out by the Israelites; the most vicious of the Wild West Bank settlers often refer to non-Jews as Amalek.

Baruch ata adonai, elohaynu melech haolum - "Blessed art thou, O Lord our God, Ruler of the Universe." The start of many prayers.

brisket - a huge, cheap cut of beef which, after being pickled or marinated, becomes pastrami, roast beef, smoked meat or, in extremely hot ovens over a long period of time, Jewish pemmican.

bubbie - grandmother.

the four questions - The Passover story begins when the youngest child at the table asks the four questions, which all begin "Why is this night different than all other nights?" and continues by pointing out that only on this night do we eat matzah; sit in a reclining position, etc. The story of the Exodus is then told as the answer.

hagaddah - book which tells the story of the Exodus, with commentary and songs; see Passover.

Hamas - depending on how you look at things, either a Palestinian charity organization attempting to raise funds for schools, orphanages and other worthy causes, or a group of terrorists whose favourite weapon, the suicide bomb, blows up with great regularity on Israeli buses. Or both. A thorn in the side of Yassir Arafat, Hamas may be Israel's own undoing — the state is said to have supported the group as a way of providing opposition to Arafat's group, Fatah.

Hezbollah - depending on how you look at things, either a group of freedom fighters trying to force the Israeli army out of the so-called security zone it occupies in southern Lebanon, or a group of terrorists backed by Iran whose favoured weapon, the Russian-made Katyusha rocket, lands with great frequency on innocent farmers in northern Israel. Or both.

Judea and Samaria - biblical names of the region known less zealously as the West Bank.

Kiryat Arba - Israeli settlement on the outskirts of Hebron.

kvetching - complaining.

matzah - unleavened bread…you know, crackers; the idea is that the former slaves fleeing Egypt had no time to sit and watch the dough rise, so the least we can do to remember their time in the desert is to eat what they did for eight days.

matzah balls - fluffy dough-like rounds that accompany chicken soup; think dumplings, but not so chewy.

Moshiach - the messiah.

Oslo Accord - secretly negotiated deal which is supposed to lead to Palestinian autonomy over the Gaza Strip and parts of the West Bank; of course, autonomy is in the eye of the beholden.

Passover - annual 8-day celebration of the Exodus from Egypt; the first two nights are dedicated to a dinner (*seder*) at which the story of Moses leading the slaves from bondage is told, the story being contained in a book known as the Haggadah, of which there are many versions. After the first two nights, the main preoccupation of those observing Passover is to figure out how to eat matzah in as many different ways as possible.

seder - Passover dinner; see Passover.

shabbas - The Jewish Sabbath, which lasts from sundown Friday to sundown Saturday; observant Jews do not work during this period.

shul - synagogue

tallis - a prayer shawl, hung around the shoulders by men once they've been bar mitzvahed. Oh come on, you know what a bar mitzvah is.

tatala - term of endearment, for a male child.

Yad Vashem - Holocaust Memorial in Israel.

yarmalke - skull cap

Yontif - any Jewish holiday

zaydie - grandfather

Other published plays by Jason Sherman...

The Retreat
ISBN 0-88754-511-4
$12.95 / Playwrights Canada Press

&

WINNER - 1995 GOVERNOR GENERAL'S LITERARY AWARD FOR DRAMA

Three in the Back, Two in the Head
ISBN 0-88754-534-3
$11.95 / Playwrights Canada Press

The League of Nathans
ISBN 0-896239-15-3 / $12.96
$12.95 / Scirocco Drama